Jeremiah 29:11

"For I know ~~the plans I~~
have for you," says the Lord.
They are plans for good and
not for disaster, to give you
hope and a future. In those
days you pray, I will listen.
If you look for me
wholeheartedly, you will find me.

W9-CFB-098

To: _Stevie Hall_

From: _The Steve Brooks Family_

A Special Message:

Congratulations
on your
2015 Graduation !

Copyright © 2015 by Worthy Inspired, a division of Worthy Media, Inc.

ISBN 978-1-61795-480-1

Published by Worthy Inspired, an imprint of Worthy Publishing Group, a division of
Worthy Media, Inc.
134 Franklin Road, Suite 200, Brentwood, Tennessee 37027.

Scripture references marked KJV are from the Holy Bible, King James Version

Scripture references marked NKJV are from the Holy Bible, New King James Version.
Copyright © 1982 by Thomas Nelson, Inc. Used by permission.

Scripture references marked NCV are from the New Century Version®. Copyright © 1987,
1988, 1991 by Word Publishing, a division of Thomas Nelson, Inc. All rights reserved. Used
by permission.

Scripture references marked HCSB are from the Holman Christian Standard Bible™
Copyright © 1999, 2000, 2001 by Holman Bible Publishers. Used by permission.

Scripture references marked NIV are from the Holy Bible, New International Version®, NIV®
Copyright © 1973, 1978, 1984, 2011 by Biblica, Inc.® Used by permission. All rights reserved
worldwide.

Scripture references marked NLT are from the Holy Bible. New Living Translation. Copyright
© 1996 Tyndale Charitable Trust. Used by permission of Tyndale House Publishers.

Scripture references marked MSG are from the Message. Copyright © 1993, 1994, 1995, 1996,
2000, 2001, 2002. Used by permission of NavPress Publishing Group.

Scripture references marked NASB are from the New American Standard Bible®, Copyright
© 1960, 1962, 1963, 1968, 1971, 1972, 1973, 1975, 1977, 1995 by The Lockman Founda-
tion. Used by permission.

All rights reserved. No part of this publication may be reproduced, stored in a retrieval
system, or transmitted in any form or by any means—electronic, mechanical, photocopy,
recording, scanning, or other—except for brief quotations in critical reviews or articles,
without the prior written permission of the publisher Freeman-Smith.

Cover Design by Kim Russell / Wahoo Designs
Page Layout by Bart Dawson

Printed in the United States of America

1 2 3 4 5—LBM—19 18 17 16 15

HERE WE GO!

GOD'S ROADMAP FOR YOU

WORTHY
Inspired

The Lord says, "Forget what happened before,
and do not think about the past.
Look at the new thing I am going to do.
It is already happening. Don't you see it?
I will make a road in the desert
and rivers in the dry land."

—

Isaiah 43:18-19 NCV

TABLE OF CONTENTS

INTRODUCTION

As you graduate into your next phase of life, you've got decisions to make . . . lots of them. And make no mistake: Your decisions are shaped by your values. Simply put, your values determine, to a surprising extent, the quality of the choices you make and the direction that your life will take. And that's why the ideas in this book are so important. This book will help you think about the values that are most important to you as you embark upon your next grand adventure.

You may find it helpful to read the book from cover to cover, or you may decide to scan the table of contents and then read to chapters that seem particularly important to you. Either way, the ideas on these pages will serve to remind you of God's commandments, God's promises, God's love, and God's Son—all are crucially important as you establish priorities for the next stage of your life's journey.

When you decide to make God's priorities your priorities, you will receive His abundance and His peace. When you make God a full partner in every aspect of your life, He will lead you along the proper path: His path. When you allow God to direct your steps, He will honor you with spiritual blessings that are simply too numerous to count. So, as you make your next important decision, pause to consider the values that serve as the starting point for that decision. When you do, your decision-making will be vastly improved . . . and so will your life.

CHAPTER 1

READY, SET, GO!

And He who sits on the throne said, "Behold, I am making all things new."

Revelation 21:5 NASB

Here you go! You've graduated from something (or somewhere) to something else (or someplace else), and you're about to embark upon your Next Big Adventure.

As you think about your future—and as you consider that countless opportunities will be woven into the fabric of the days ahead—be sure to include God in your plans. When you do, He will guide your steps and light your path.

Perhaps you desire to change the direction of your life, or perhaps you're determined to make major modifications in the way you live or the way you think. If so, you and God, working together, can do it. But don't expect change to be easy or instant. God expects you to do your fair share of the work—and that's as it should be. Nonetheless, if you trust the Father completely, and if you don't give up, you're destined to accomplish big things . . . very big things.

If you're going through a spiritual growth spurt, don't be surprised if you experience a few spiritual growing pains.

Why? Because real transformation begins on the inside and works it's way out from there. And sometimes, the "working out" is painful.

Lasting change doesn't occur "out there"; it occurs "in here." It occurs, not in the shifting sands of your own particular circumstances, but in the quiet depths of your own obedient heart. So if you're in search of a new beginning or, for that matter, a new you, don't expect changing circumstances to miraculously transform you into the person you want to become. Transformation starts with God, and it starts in the silent center of a humble human heart—like yours.

God has a roadmap for your life, a plan that's designed precisely for you. If you seek His guidance, He'll direct your steps; He'll help carry your burdens; and, He'll help you focus on the things that really matter.

God is not running an antique shop! He is making all things new!

Vance Havner

The amazing thing about Jesus is that He doesn't just patch up our lives, He gives us a brand new sheet, a clean slate to start over, all new.

Gloria Gaither

Like a spring of pure water, God's peace in our hearts brings cleansing and refreshment to our minds and bodies.

Billy Graham

Whoever you are, whatever your condition or circumstance, whatever your past or problem, Jesus can restore you to wholeness.

Anne Graham Lotz

Walking with God leads to receiving his intimate counsel, and counseling leads to deep restoration.

John Eldredge

No matter how badly we have failed, we can always get up and begin again. Our God is the God of new beginnings.

Warren Wiersbe

More from God's Word about New Beginnings

But those who wait on the Lord shall renew their strength; they shall mount up with wings like eagles, they shall run and not be weary, they shall walk and not faint.

Isaiah 40:31 NKJV

Therefore if any man be in Christ, he is a new creature: old things are passed away; behold, all things are become new.

2 Corinthians 5:17 KJV

I will give you a new heart and put a new spirit within you.

Ezekiel 36:26 HCSB

Notes to Yourself about Your New Beginnings

_____

_____

_____

_____

_____

_____

_____

CHAPTER 2

PRIORITIES FOR LIFE

But whoever listens to me will live securely and be free from the fear of danger.

Proverbs 1:33 HCSB

As you graduate into the next phase of life, remember this: Everything on your to-do list is not created equal. Certain tasks are extremely important while others are not. Therefore, it's important to prioritize your daily activities and complete each task in the approximate order of its importance.

The principle of doing first things first is simple in theory but more complicated in practice. Well-meaning family, friends, and coworkers have a way of making unexpected demands upon your time. Furthermore, each day has it own share of minor emergencies; these urgent matters tend to draw your attention away from more important ones. On paper, prioritizing is simple, but to act upon those priorities in the real world requires maturity, patience, determination, and balance.

If you fail to prioritize your day, life will automatically do the job for you. So your choice is simple: prioritize or be prioritized. It's a choice that will help determine the quality of your life.

Are you living a balanced life that allows time for worship, for family, for school, for exercise, and a little time left over for you? Or do you feel overworked, under appreciated, and overwhelmed? If your to-do list is "maxed out" and your energy is on the wane, it's time to restore a sense of balance to your life. You can do so by turning the concerns and the priorities of this day over to God—prayerfully, earnestly, and often. Then, you must listen for His answer . . . and trust the answer He gives.

As you begin anew, be sure to make time for God. Even if your day is filled to the brim with obligations and priorities, but no priority is greater than our obligation to our Creator. Make sure to give Him the time He deserves, not only on Sundays, but also on every other day of the week.

Great relief and satisfaction can come from seeking God's priorities for us in each season, discerning what is "best" in the midst of many noble opportunities, and pouring our most excellent energies into those things.

Beth Moore

Setting goals is one way you can be sure that you will focus your efforts on the main things so that trivial matters will not become your focus.

Charles Stanley

Give me the person who says, "This one thing I do, and not these fifty things I dabble in."

D. L. Moody

The work of God is appointed. There is always enough time to do the will of God.

Elisabeth Elliot

The moment you wake up each morning, all your wishes and hopes for the day rush at you like wild animals. And the first job each morning consists in shoving it all back; in listening to that other voice, taking that other point of view, letting that other, larger, stronger, quieter life coming flowing in.

C. S. Lewis

More from God's Word about Priorities

And I pray this: that your love will keep on growing in knowledge and every kind of discernment, so that you can determine what really matters and can be pure and blameless in the day of Christ.

Philippians 1:9 HCSB

So teach us to number our days, that we may gain a heart of wisdom.

Psalm 90:12 NKJV

For where your treasure is, there will your heart be also.

Luke 12:34 KJV

Notes to Yourself about Your Priorities

_____

_____

_____

_____

_____

_____

_____

CHAPTER 3

WISDOM ACCORDING TO GOD

I will instruct you and show you the way to go; with My eye on you, I will give counsel.

Psalm 32:8 HCSB

Do you place a high value on the acquisition of wisdom? If so, you are not alone; most people would like to be wise, but not everyone is willing to do the work that is required to become wise. Wisdom is not like a mushroom; it does not spring up overnight. It is, instead, like an oak tree that starts as a tiny acorn, grows into a sapling, and eventually reaches up to the sky, tall and strong.

To become wise, you must seek God's guidance and live according to His Word. To become wise, you must seek instruction with consistency and purpose. To become wise, you must not only learn the lessons of the Christian life, but you must also live by them. But oftentimes, that's easier said than done.

Sometimes, amid the demands of daily life, you will lose perspective. Life may seem out of balance, and the pressures of everyday living may seem overwhelming. What's needed is a fresh perspective, a restored sense of balance . . . and God's wisdom. If you call upon the Lord and seek to see the world through His eyes, He will give you guidance, wisdom and perspective. When you make God's priorities your priorities, He will lead you according to His plan and according to His commandments. When you study God's teachings, you are reminded that God's reality is the ultimate reality.

Do you seek to live a life of righteousness and wisdom? If so, you must study the ultimate source of wisdom: the Word of God. You must seek out worthy mentors and listen carefully to their advice. You must associate, day in and day out, with godly men and women. Then, as you accumulate wisdom, you must not keep it for yourself; you must, instead, share it with your friends and family members.

But be forewarned: if you sincerely seek to share your hard-earned wisdom with others, your actions must reflect the values that you hold dear. The best way to share your wisdom is not by your words, but by your example.

Need wisdom? God's got it. If you want it, then study God's Word and associate with godly people.

If we neglect the Bible, we cannot expect to benefit from the wisdom and direction that result from knowing God's Word.

Vonette Bright

No matter how many books you read, no matter how many schools you attend, you're never really wise until you start making wise choices.

Marie T. Freeman

The man who prays ceases to be a fool.

Oswald Chambers

The fruit of wisdom is Christlikeness, peace, humility, and love. And, the root of it is faith in Christ as the manifested wisdom of God.

J. I. Packer

Having a doctrine pass before the mind is not what the Bible means by knowing the truth. It's only when it reaches down deep into the heart that the truth begins to set us free, just as a key must penetrate a lock to turn it, or as rainfall must saturate the earth down to the roots in order for your garden to grow.

John Eldredge

More from God's Word about Wisdom

So teach us to number our days, that we may gain a heart of wisdom.

Psalm 90:12 NKJV

Teach me, O Lord, the way of Your statutes, and I shall keep it to the end.

Psalm 119:33 NKJV

A wise man will hear and increase learning, and a man of understanding will attain wise counsel.

Proverbs 1:5 NKJV

 ### Notes to Yourself about How to Gain Wisdom

_____

_____

_____

_____

_____

_____

_____

CHAPTER 4

LET GOD'S ROADMAP DIRECT YOUR THOUGHTS

Finally brothers, whatever is true, whatever is honorable, whatever is just, whatever is pure, whatever is lovely, whatever is commendable—if there is any moral excellence and if there is any praise—dwell on these things.

Philippians 4:8 HCSB

Our thoughts have the power to shape our lives—for better or worse. Thoughts have the power to lift our spirits, to improve our circumstances, and to strengthen our relationship with the Creator. But, our thoughts also have the power to cause us great harm if we focus too intently upon those things that distance us from God.

How will you direct your thoughts today? Will you obey the words of Philippians 4:8 by dwelling upon those things that are honorable, true, and worthy of praise? Or will you allow your thoughts to be hijacked by the negativity that seems to dominate our troubled world?

Are you fearful, angry, bored, or worried? Are you so preoccupied with the concerns of this day that you fail to thank

God for the promise of eternity? Are you confused, bitter, or pessimistic? If so, God wants to have a little talk with you.

As you make the journey through life, God intends that you experience joy and abundance, but He will not force His joy upon you; you must claim it for yourself. It's up to you to celebrate the life that God has given you by focusing your mind upon "whatever is of good repute." Today, spend more time thinking about your blessings, and less time fretting about your hardships. Then, take time to thank the Giver of all things good for gifts that are, in truth, far too numerous to count.

Good thoughts create good deeds. Good thoughts lead to good deeds and bad thoughts lead elsewhere. So guard your thoughts accordingly.

Attitude is the mind's paintbrush; it can color any situation.

Barbara Johnson

People who do not develop and practice good thinking often find themselves at the mercy of their circumstances.

John Maxwell

Your thoughts are the determining factor as to whose mold you are conformed to. Control your thoughts and you control the direction of your life.

Charles Stanley

The things we think are the things that feed our souls. If we think on pure and lovely things, we shall grow pure and lovely like them; and the converse is equally true.

Hannah Whitall Smith

If our minds are stayed upon God, His peace will rule the affairs entertained by our minds. If, on the other hand, we allow our minds to dwell on the cares of this world, God's peace will be far from our thoughts.

Woodroll Kroll

More from God's Word about Your Thoughts

Set your mind on things above, not on things on the earth.

Colossians 3:2 NKJV

Commit your works to the Lord, and your thoughts will be established.

Proverbs 16:3 NKJV

Guard your heart above all else, for it is the source of life.

Proverbs 4:23 HCSB

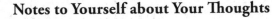

Notes to Yourself about Your Thoughts

_____

_____

_____

_____

_____

_____

_____

_____

_____

CHAPTER 5

THE REWARDS OF FOLLOWING GOD'S ROADMAP

For the eyes of the Lord are on the righteous, and His ears are open to their prayers; but the face of the Lord is against those who do evil.

1 Peter 3:12 NKJV

As you embark upon the next stage of your life's journey, do you want to be successful and happy? If so, be sure to use God's roadmap. When you're faced with a difficult choice or a powerful temptation, pray about it. Invite God into your heart and live according to His commandments. When you do, you will be blessed today, and tomorrow, and forever.

Each new day presents countless opportunities to put God in first place . . . or not. When we honor Him by living according to His commandments, we earn for ourselves the abundance and peace that He promises. But, when we concern ourselves more with pleasing others than with pleasing our Creator, we bring needless suffering upon ourselves and our families. Would you like a time-tested formula for successful living? Here is a formula that is proven and true: Seek God's approval in every aspect of your life. Does this sound too simple? Perhaps it is simple, but it is also the only way to reap the marvelous riches that God has in store for you.

So today, take every step of your journey with God as your traveling companion. Read His Word and follow His commandments. Support only those activities that further God's kingdom and your own spiritual growth. Then, reap the blessings that God has promised to all those who live according to His will and His Word.

Righteous living leads to joy. Bill Hybels observes, "Christianity says we were created by a righteous God to flourish and be exhilarated in a righteous environment. God has 'wired' us in such a way that the more righteous we are, the more we'll actually enjoy life." Holy living doesn't take the joy out of life, it puts it in.

Let us never suppose that obedience is impossible or that holiness is meant only for a select few. Our Shepherd leads us in paths of righteousness—not for our name's sake but for His.

Elisabeth Elliot

We must appropriate the tender mercy of God every day after conversion, or problems quickly develop. We need his grace daily in order to live a righteous life.

Jim Cymbala

When we do what is right, we have contentment, peace, and happiness.

Beverly LaHaye

Righteousness not only defines God, but God defines righteousness.

Bill Hybels

A life growing in its purity and devotion will be a more prayerful life.

E. M. Bounds

Our progress in holiness depends on God and ourselves—on God's grace and on our will to be holy.

Mother Teresa

More from God's Word about Righteousness

Sow righteousness for yourselves and reap faithful love; break up your untilled ground. It is time to seek the Lord until He comes and sends righteousness on you like the rain.

Hosea 10:12 HCSB

And the world is passing away, and the lust of it; but he who does the will of God abides forever.

1 John 2:17 NKJV

The righteous one will live by his faith.

Habakkuk 2:4 HCSB

Notes to Yourself about Righteousness

_____

_____

_____

_____

_____

_____

CHAPTER 6

DISCOVERING HIS PEACE

Peace I leave with you, My peace I give to you; not as the world gives do I give to you. Let not your heart be troubled, neither let it be afraid.

John 14:27 NKJV

Oftentimes, our outer struggles are simply manifestations of the inner conflict that we feel when we stray from God's path. The beautiful words of John 14:27 remind us that Jesus offers us peace, not as the world gives, but as He alone gives. Our challenge is to accept Christ's peace into our hearts and then, as best we can, to share His peace with our neighbors. When we accept Jesus as our personal Savior, we are transformed by His grace. We are then free to accept the spiritual abundance and peace that can be ours through the power of the risen Christ.

Have you found the genuine peace that can be yours through Jesus Christ? Or are you still rushing after the illusion of "peace and happiness" that the world promises but cannot deliver? Today, as a gift to yourself, to your family, and to your friends, claim the inner peace that is your spiritual birthright: the peace of Jesus Christ. It is offered freely; it has been paid for in full; it is yours for the asking. So ask. And then share.

God's peace surpasses human understanding. When you accept His peace, it will revolutionize your life.

In the center of a hurricane there is
absolute quiet and peace.
There is no safer place
than in the center of the will of God.

—

Corrie ten Boom

A great many people are trying to make peace, but that has already been done. God has not left it for us to do; all we have to do is to enter into it.

D. L. Moody

There may be no trumpet sound or loud applause when we make a right decision, just a calm sense of resolution and peace.

Gloria Gaither

What peace can they have who are not at peace with God?

Matthew Henry

God is in control of history; it's His story. Doesn't that give you a great peace—especially when world events seem so tumultuous and insane?

Kay Arthur

First keep the peace within yourself, then you can also bring peace to others.

Thomas à Kempis

More from God's Word about Peace

God has called us to peace.

1 Corinthians 7:15 NKJV

In this world you will have trouble. But take heart! I have overcome the world.

John 16:33 NIV

Be of good comfort, be of one mind, live in peace; and the God of love and peace will be with you.

2 Corinthians 13:11 NKJV

Notes to Yourself about How to Find Peace

_____

_____

_____

_____

_____

_____

_____

CHAPTER 7

THE WISDOM OF THANKSGIVING

In everything give thanks; for this is the will of God in Christ Jesus for you.

1 Thessalonians 5:18 NKJV

As Christians, we are blessed beyond measure. God sent his only Son to die for our sins. And, God has given us the priceless gifts of eternal love and eternal life. We, in turn, are instructed to approach our Heavenly Father with reverence and thanksgiving. But sometimes, in the crush of everyday living, we simply don't stop long enough to pause and thank our Creator for the countless blessings He has bestowed upon us.

When we slow down and express our gratitude to the One who made us, we enrich our own lives and the lives of those around us. Thanksgiving should become a habit, a regular part of our daily routines. God has blessed us beyond measure, and we owe Him everything, including our eternal praise.

Are you a thankful person? Do you appreciate the gifts that God has given you? And, do you demonstrate your gratitude by being a faithful steward of the gifts and talents that you have received from your Creator? You most certainly should be thankful. After all, when you stop to think about it, God has given you more blessings than you can count. So the question of the day is this: will you thank your Heavenly Father . . . or will you spend your time and energy doing other things?

God is always listening—are you willing to say thanks? It's up to you, and the next move is yours.

You owe God everything . . .
including your thanks.

Thanksgiving is good but Thanksliving is better.

Jim Gallery

If you can't tell whether your glass is half-empty or half-full, you don't need another glass; what you need is better eyesight . . . and a more thankful heart.

Marie T. Freeman

The joy of the Holy Spirit is experienced by giving thanks in all situations.

Bill Bright

The ability to rejoice in any situation is a sign of spiritual maturity.

Billy Graham

Thanksgiving or complaining—these words express two contrastive attitudes of the souls of God's children in regard to His dealings with them. The soul that gives thanks can find comfort in everything; the soul that complains can find comfort in nothing.

Hannah Whitall Smith

41

More from God's Word about Thanksgiving

Thanks be to God for His indescribable gift.

2 Corinthians 9:15 HCSB

Therefore as you have received Christ Jesus the Lord, walk in Him, rooted and built up in Him and established in the faith, just as you were taught, and overflowing with thankfulness.

Colossians 2:6-7 HCSB

It is good to give thanks to the Lord, and to sing praises to Your name, O Most High.

Psalm 92:1 NKJV

Notes to Yourself about Your Blessings

CHAPTER 8

USE YOUR GIFTS

Do not neglect the gift that is in you.

1 Timothy 4:14 NKJV

God knew precisely what He was doing when He gave you a unique set of talents and opportunities. And now, God wants you to use those talents for the glory of His kingdom. So here's the big question: will you choose to use those talents, or not?

Your Heavenly Father wants you to be a faithful steward of the gifts He has given you. But you live in a society that may encourage you to do otherwise. You face countless temptations to squander your time, your resources, and your talents. So you must be keenly aware of the inevitable distractions that can waste your time, your energy, and your opportunities.

Every day of your life, you have a choice to make: to nurture your talents or neglect them. When you choose wisely, God rewards your efforts, and He expands your opportunities to serve Him.

God has blessed you with unique opportunities to serve Him, and He has given you every tool that you need to do so. Today, accept this challenge: value the talent that God has given you, nourish it, make it grow, and share it with the world. After all, the best way to say "Thank You" for God's gifts is to use them.

Polishing your skills requires effort: Converting raw talent into polished skill usually requires work, and lots of it. God's Word clearly instructs you to do the hard work of refining your talents for the glory of His kingdom and the service of His people. So, we are wise to remember the old adage: "What you are is God's gift to you; what you become is your gift to God." And it's up to you to make sure that your gift is worthy of the Giver.

Not everyone possesses boundless energy or a conspicuous talent. We are not equally blessed with great intellect or physical beauty or emotional strength. But we have all been given the same ability to be faithful.

Gigi Graham Tchividjian

God has given you special talents—now it's your turn to give them back to God.

Marie T. Freeman

If you want to reach your potential, you need to add a strong work ethic to your talent.

John Maxwell

You are the only person on earth who can use your ability.

Zig Ziglar

In the great orchestra we call life, you have an instrument and a song, and you owe it to God to play them both sublimely.

Max Lucado

More from God's Word about Talents

Each one has his own gift from God, one in this manner and another in that.

1 Corinthians 7:7 NKJV

I remind you to keep ablaze the gift of God that is in you.

2 Timothy 1:6 HCSB

God has given gifts to each of you from his great variety of spiritual gifts. Manage them well so that God's generosity can flow through you.

1 Peter 4:10 NLT

 ## Notes to Yourself about Using Your Talents

_____

_____

_____

_____

_____

_____

CHAPTER 9

LIFE WITH A CAPITAL "L"

Do all you can to live a peaceful life. Take care of your own business, and do your own work as we have already told you. If you do, then people who are not believers will respect you, and you will not have to depend on others for what you need.

1 Thessalonians 4:11-12 NCV

Life can tough sometimes, but it's also wonderful—and it's a glorious gift from God. How will you use that gift? Will you treat this day as a precious treasure from your Heavenly Father, or will you take the next 24 hours for granted? The answer should be obvious: Every day, including this one, comes gift-wrapped from God—your job is unwrap that gift, to use it wisely, and to give thanks to the Giver.

Instead of sleepwalking through life, you must wake up and live in the precious present. Each waking moment holds the potential to celebrate, to serve, to share, or to love. Because you are a person with incalculable potential, each moment has incalculable value. Your challenge is to experience each day to the full as you seek to live in accordance with

God's plan for your life. When you do, you'll experience His abundance and His peace.

Are you willing to treat this day (and every one hereafter) as a special gift to be savored and celebrated? You should—and if you seek to Live with a capital L, you most certainly will.

Be a realistic optimist about life, and remember that your attitude toward the future will help create your future. You might as well put the self-fulfilling prophecy to work for you, and besides, life is far too short to be a pessimist.

The Bible says that being a Christian is not only a great way to die, but it's also the best way to live.

Bill Hybels

God's riches are beyond anything we could ask or even dare to imagine! If my life gets gooey and stale, I have no excuse.

Barbara Johnson

You've heard the saying, "Life is what you make it." That means we have a choice. We can choose to have a life full of frustration and fear, but we can just as easily choose one of joy and contentment.

Dennis Swanberg

Wherever you are, be all there. Live to the hilt every situation you believe to be the will of God.

Jim Elliot

Life is not a holiday, but an education. And the one eternal lesson for us all is how better we can love.

Henry Drummond

More from God's Word about Life

I urge you now to live the life to which God called you.

Ephesians 4:1 NKJV

Shout triumphantly to the Lord, all the earth. Serve the Lord with gladness; come before Him with joyful songs.

Psalm 100:1-2 HCSB

Rejoice in the Lord always. Again I will say, rejoice!

Philippians 4:4 NKJV

Notes to Yourself about Ways to Improve Your Life

_____

_____

_____

_____

_____

_____

_____

CHAPTER 10

AND THE GREATEST OF THESE . . .

Though I speak with the tongues of men and of angels, but have not love, I have become sounding brass or a clanging cymbal.

1 Corinthians 13:1 NKJV

L ove, like everything else in this wonderful world, begins and ends with God, but the middle part belongs to us. During the brief time that we have here on earth, God has given each of us the opportunity to become a loving person—or not. God has given each of us the opportunity to be kind, to be courteous, to be cooperative, and to be forgiving—or not. God has given each of us the chance to obey the Golden Rule, or to make up our own rules as we go. If we obey God's rules, we're safe, but if we do otherwise, we're headed for trouble in a hurry.

There's an old saying that's both trite and true: If you aren't loving, you aren't living. But here in the real world, it isn't always easy to love other people, especially when those people have done things to hurt you. Still, God's Word is clear: you are instructed to love others despite their imperfections.

God does not intend for you to experience mediocre relationships; He created you for far greater things. Building lasting relationships requires compassion, wisdom, empathy, kindness, courtesy, and forgiveness. If that sounds a lot like work, it is—which is perfectly fine with God. Why? Because He knows that you are capable of doing that work, and because He knows that the fruits of your labors will enrich the lives of your loved ones and the lives of generations yet unborn.

Love at first sight always deserves a second look. If you give your heart away too easily or too often, you may find that it is returned you . . . in very poor condition!

Only God can give us a selfless love for others, as the Holy Spirit changes us from within.

Billy Graham

Truth becomes hard if it is not softened by love, and love becomes soft if not strengthened by truth.

E. Stanley Jones

We long to find someone who has been where we've been, who shares our fragile skies, who sees our sunsets with the same shades of blue.

Beth Moore

How much a person loves someone is obvious by how much he is willing to sacrifice for that person.

Bill Bright

The truth of the Gospel is intended to free us to love God and others with our whole heart.

John Eldredge

More from God's Word about Love

Now these three remain: faith, hope, and love. But the greatest of these is love.

1 Corinthians 13:13 HCSB

Beloved, if God so loved us, we also ought to love one another.

1 John 4:11 NKJV

Love is patient; love is kind. Love does not envy; is not boastful; is not conceited; does not act improperly; is not selfish; is not provoked; does not keep a record of wrongs; finds no joy in unrighteousness, but rejoices in the truth; bears all things,

1 Corinthians 13:4-7 HCSB

 ## Notes to Yourself about the Importance of Love

_____

_____

_____

_____

_____

_____

CHAPTER 11

THE JOURNEY TOWARD SPIRITUAL MATURITY

But grow in the grace and knowledge of our Lord and Savior Jesus Christ. To Him be the glory both now and to the day of eternity.

2 Peter 3:18 HCSB

As you graduate into the next phase of your life's journey, remember this: When it comes to your faith, God doesn't intend for you to stand still. He wants you to keep moving and growing. In fact, God's plan for you includes a lifetime of prayer, praise, and spiritual growth.

When we cease to grow, either emotionally or spiritually, we do ourselves and our loved ones a profound disservice. But, if we study God's Word, if we obey His commandments, and if we live in the center of His will, we will not be "stagnant" believers; we will, instead, be growing Christians . . . and that's exactly what God wants for our lives.

Many of life's most important lessons are painful to learn. During times of heartbreak and hardship, we must be courageous and we must be patient, knowing that in His own time, God will heal us if we invite Him into our hearts.

Spiritual growth need not take place only in times of adversity. We must seek to grow in our knowledge and love of the Lord every day that we live. In those quiet moments when we open our hearts to God, the One who made us keeps remaking us. He gives us direction, perspective, wisdom, and courage. The appropriate moment to accept those spiritual gifts is the present one.

Are you as mature as you're ever going to be? Hopefully not! When it comes to your faith, God doesn't intend for you to become "fully grown," at least not in this lifetime. In fact, God still has important lessons that He intends to teach you. So ask yourself this: what lesson is God trying to teach me today? And then go about the business of learning it.

Spiritual maturity is a journey, not a destination. And the sooner you begin that journey, the farther you're likely to go.

I'm not what I want to be. I'm not what I'm going to be. But, thank God, I'm not what I was!

Gloria Gaither

Enjoy the adventure of receiving God's guidance. Taste it, revel in it, appreciate the fact that the journey is often a lot more exciting than arriving at the destination.

Bill Hybels

Some people have received Christ but have never reached spiritual maturity. We should grow as Christians every day, and we are not completely mature until we live in the presence of Christ.

Billy Graham

I've never met anyone who became instantly mature. It's a painstaking process that God takes us through, and it includes such things as waiting, failing, losing, and being misunderstood—each calling for extra doses of perseverance.

Charles Swindoll

More from God's Word about Spiritual Growth

Therefore, leaving the elementary message about the Messiah, let us go on to maturity.

Hebrews 6:1 HCSB

May the God of hope fill you with all joy and peace as you trust in him, so that you may overflow with hope by the power of the Holy Spirit.

Romans 15:13 NIV

Create in me a clean heart, O God; and renew a right spirit within me.

Psalm 51:10 KJV

 Notes to Yourself about Your Own Spiritual Growth

_____

_____

_____

_____

_____

CHAPTER 12

BE CHEERFUL

Jacob said, "For what a relief it is to see your friendly smile. It is like seeing the smile of God!"

Genesis 33:10 NLT

Cheerfulness is a gift that we give to others and to our-selves. And, as believers who have been saved by a risen Christ, why shouldn't we be cheerful? The answer, of course, is that we have every reason to honor our Savior with joy in our hearts, smiles on our faces, and words of celebration on our lips.

Few things in life are more sad, or, for that matter, more absurd, than grumpy Christians. Christ promises us lives of abundance and joy if we accept His love and His grace. Yet sometimes, even the most righteous among us are beset by fits of ill temper and frustration. During these moments, we may not feel like turning our thoughts and prayers to Christ, but if we seek to gain perspective and peace, that's precisely what we must do.

How cheerful are you? Do you spend most of your day celebrating your life or complaining about it? If you're a big-time celebrator, keep celebrating. But if you've established the bad habit of looking at the hole instead of the donut, it's time to correct your spiritual vision.

Pessimism and doubt are two of the most important tools that the devil uses to achieve his objectives. Your challenge, of course, is to ensure that Satan cannot use these tools on you. So today, make sure to celebrate the life that God has given you. Your Creator has blessed you beyond measure. Honor Him with your prayers, your words, your deeds, and your joy.

Do you need a little cheering up? If so, find somebody else who needs cheering up, too. Then, do your best to brighten that person's day. When you do, you'll discover that cheering up other people is a wonderful way to cheer yourself up, too!

It is not fitting, when one is in God's service, to have a gloomy face or a chilling look.

St. Francis of Assisi

God is good, and heaven is forever. And if those two facts don't cheer you up, nothing will.

Marie T. Freeman

We may run, walk, stumble, drive, or fly, but let us never lose sight of the reason for the journey, or miss a chance to see a rainbow on the way.

Gloria Gaither

Be assured, my dear friend, that it is no joy to God in seeing you with a dreary countenance.

C. H. Spurgeon

When we bring sunshine into the lives of others, we're warmed by it ourselves. When we spill a little happiness, it splashes on us.

Barbara Johnson

More from God's Word about Cheerfulness

A merry heart does good, like medicine.

Proverbs 17:22 NKJV

Is anyone cheerful? He should sing praises.

James 5:13 HCSB

A cheerful look brings joy to the heart, and good news gives health to the bones.

Proverbs 15:30 NIV

Notes to Yourself about the Rewards of Being a Cheerful Person

_____

_____

_____

_____

_____

_____

_____

CHAPTER 13

THE POWER OF HOPE

You have already heard about this hope in the message of truth, the gospel that has come to you. It is bearing fruit and growing all over the world, just as it has among you since the day you heard it and recognized God's grace in the truth.

Colossians 1:5-6 HCSB

There are few sadder sights on earth than the sight of a person who has lost hope. In difficult times, hope can be elusive, but those who place their faith in God's promises need never lose it. After all, God is good; His love endures; He has promised His children the gift of eternal life. And, God keeps His promises.

Despite God's promises, despite Christ's love, and despite our countless blessings, we're only human, and we can still lose hope from time to time. When we do, we need the encouragement of Christian friends, the life-changing power of prayer, and the healing truth of God's Holy Word.

If you find yourself falling into the spiritual traps of worry and discouragement, seek the healing touch of Jesus and the encouraging words of fellow believers. And if you find a friend in need, remind him or her of the peace that is found through a genuine relationship with Christ. It was Christ who promised, "I have told you these things so that in Me you may have peace. In the world you have suffering. But take courage! I have conquered the world" (John 16:33 HCSB). This world can be a place of trials and troubles, but as believers, we are secure. God has promised us peace, joy, and eternal life. And, of course, God keeps His promises today, tomorrow, and forever.

Never be afraid to hope—
or to ask—for a miracle.

Hope is a wonderful thing—one little nibble will keep a man fishing all day.

Barbara Johnson

Easter comes each year to remind us of a truth that is eternal and universal. The empty tomb of Easter morning says to you and me, "Of course you'll encounter trouble. But behold a God of power who can take any evil and turn it into a door of hope."

Catherine Marshall

The hope we have in Jesus is the anchor for the soul— something sure and steadfast, preventing drifting or giving way, lowered to the depth of God's love.

Franklin Graham

Love is the seed of all hope. It is the enticement to trust, to risk, to try, and to go on.

Gloria Gaither

God's people have always tied their lives to a single hope, the assurance of one day seeing God in heaven.

Warren Wiersbe

More from God's Word about Hope

Let us hold on to the confession of our hope without wavering, for He who promised is faithful.

Hebrews 10:23 HCSB

Sustain me according to Your word, that I may live; and do not let me be ashamed of my hope.

Psalm 119:116 NASB

I wait for the Lord; I wait, and put my hope in His word.

Psalm 130:5 HCSB

 ## Notes to Yourself about the Value of Hope

CHAPTER 14

OPPORTUNITIES EVERYWHERE

Therefore, as we have opportunity, we must work for the good of all, especially for those who belong to the household of faith.

Galatians 6:10 HCSB

As you travel through life, do you see opportunities, possibilities, and blessings, or do you focus, instead, upon the more negative scenery? Do you spend more time counting your blessings or your misfortunes? If you've acquired the unfortunate habit of focusing too intently upon the negative aspects of life, then your spiritual vision is in need of correction.

Whether you realize it or not, opportunities are whirling around you like stars crossing the night sky: beautiful to observe, but too numerous to count. Yet you may be too concerned with the challenges of everyday living to notice those opportunities. That's why you should slow down occasionally, catch your breath, and focus your thoughts on two things: the talents God has given you and the opportunities that He has placed before you. God is leading you in the direction of those opportunities. Your task is to watch carefully, to pray fervently, and to act accordingly.

Are you willing to place your future in the hands of a loving and all-knowing God? Do you trust in the ultimate goodness of His plan for your life? Will you face today's challenges with optimism and hope? You should. After all, God created you for a very important purpose: His purpose. And you still have important work to do: His work. And the time to start doing that work is now.

Familiarize yourself with the opportunities of tomorrow. Tomorrow is filled with opportunities for people who are willing to find them and work for them. So make certain that you have more than a passing familiarity with ever shifting sands of our changing world.

Worry is the senseless process of cluttering up tomorrow's opportunities with leftover problems from today.

Barbara Johnson

Life is a glorious opportunity.

Billy Graham

We are all faced with a series of great opportunities, brilliantly disguised as unsolvable problems. Unsolvable without God's wisdom, that is.

Charles Swindoll

God specializes in things fresh and firsthand. His plans for you this year may outshine those of the past. He's prepared to fill your days with reasons to give Him praise.

Joni Eareckson Tada

Keep your feet on the ground, but let your heart soar as high as it will. Refuse to be average or to surrender to the chill of your spiritual environment.

A. W. Tozer

More from God's Word about Opportunities

But Jesus looked at them and said, "With men this is impossible, but with God all things are possible."

Matthew 19:26 HCSB

For God has not given us a spirit of fearfulness, but one of power, love, and sound judgment.

2 Timothy 1:7 HCSB

I am able to do all things through Him who strengthens me.

Philippians 4:13 HCSB

 ## Notes to Yourself about Your Opportunities

_____

_____

_____

_____

_____

_____

_____

CHAPTER 15

LIVING ON PURPOSE

Whatever you do, do all to the glory of God.

1 Corinthians 10:31 NKJV

Every phase of life is best lived on purpose, not by accident: The sooner we discover what God intends for us to do with our lives, the better. But God's purposes aren't always clear to us. Sometimes we wander aimlessly in a wilderness of our own making. And sometimes, we struggle mightily against God in a vain effort to find success and happiness through our own means, not His.

Whenever we struggle against God's plans, we suffer. When we resist God's calling, our efforts bear little fruit. Our best strategy, therefore, is to seek God's wisdom and to follow Him wherever He chooses to lead. When we do so, we are blessed.

When we align ourselves with God's purposes, we avail ourselves of His power and His peace. But how can we know precisely what God's intentions are? The answer, of course, is that even the most well-intentioned believers face periods of uncertainty and doubt about the direction of their lives. So, too, will you.

When you arrive at one of life's inevitable crossroads, that is precisely the moment when you should turn your thoughts and prayers toward God. When you do, He will make Himself known to you in a time and manner of His choosing.

Are you earnestly seeking to discern God's purpose for your life? If so, remember this: (1) God has a plan for your life; (2) If you seek that plan sincerely and prayerfully, you will find it; (3) When you discover God's purpose for your life, you will experience abundance, peace, joy, and power—God's power. And that's the only kind of power that really matters.

Discovering God's purpose for your life requires a willingness to be open. God's plan is unfolding day by day. If you keep your eyes and your heart open, He'll reveal His plans. God has big things in store for you, but He may have quite a few lessons to teach you before you are fully prepared to do His will and fulfill His purposes.

Yesterday is just experience but tomorrow is glistening with purpose—and today is the channel leading from one to the other.

Barbara Johnson

Only God's chosen task for you will ultimately satisfy. Do not wait until it is too late to realize the privilege of serving Him in His chosen position for you.

Beth Moore

It's incredible to realize that what we do each day has meaning in the big picture of God's plan.

Bill Hybels

Aim at Heaven and you will get earth "thrown in"; aim at earth and you will get neither.

C. S. Lewis

Until your purpose lines up with God's purpose, you will never be happy or fulfilled.

Charles Stanley

More from God's Word about Purpose

It is God who is at work in you, both to will and to work for His good pleasure.

Philippians 2:13 NASB

We know that all things work together for the good of those who love God: those who are called according to His purpose.

Romans 8:28 HCSB

I will instruct you and teach you in the way you should go; I will guide you with My eye.

Psalm 32:8 NKJV

Notes to Yourself about Your Purpose for Being Here

_____

_____

_____

_____

_____

_____

CHAPTER 16

BE A CHEERFUL GIVER

As each one has received a gift, minister it to one another, as good stewards of the manifold grace of God.

1 Peter 4:10 NKJV

Your blessings from God are too numerous to count. Those blessings include life, family, friends, talents, and possessions, for starters. But, your greatest blessing—a gift that is yours for the asking—is God's gift of salvation through Christ Jesus. Today, give thanks for your blessings and show your thanks by using them and by sharing them.

The thread of generosity is woven—completely and inextricably—into the very fabric of Christ's teachings. He reminded His followers that, "Whatever you did for one of the least of these brothers of mine, you did for me" (Matthew 25:40 NIV). The implication is clear: If we genuinely seek to follow Christ, we must share our time, our possessions, our love, and our faith.

Today, as you go about the business of living your life, be more generous than necessary. This world needs every bit of kindness and generosity that springs from the hearts of believers like you. Your generosity will glorify the One who has been so generous to you, and your kindness will touch the hearts of friends and strangers alike. And, be assured that no good deed is ever wasted. Every time that you share a kind word or a generous gift with another human being, you have also shared it with the Savior of the world.

There is a direct relationship between generosity and joy—the more you give to others, the more joy you will experience for yourself.

All the blessings we enjoy are divine deposits, committed to our trust on this condition: that they should be dispensed for the benefit of our neighbors.

John Calvin

Nothing is really ours until we share it.

C. S. Lewis

God does not supply money to satisfy our every whim and desire. His promise is to meet our needs and provide an abundance so that we can help other people.

Larry Burkett

The mark of a Christian is that he will walk the second mile and turn the other cheek. A wise man or woman gives the extra effort, all for the glory of the Lord Jesus Christ.

John Maxwell

The measure of a life, after all, is not its duration but its donation.

Corrie ten Boom

More from God's Word about Giving

So let each one give as he purposes in his heart, not grudgingly or of necessity; for God loves a cheerful giver.

2 Corinthians 9:7 NKJV

Dear friend, you are showing your faith by whatever you do for the brothers, and this you are doing for strangers.

3 John 1:5 HCSB

Bear one another's burdens, and so fulfill the law of Christ.

Galatians 6:2 NKJV

Notes to Yourself about the Importance of Giving

_____

_____

_____

_____

_____

_____

CHAPTER 17

MOUNTAIN-MOVING FAITH

Be on guard. Stand true to what you believe. Be courageous. Be strong.

1 Corinthians 16:13 NLT

Because we live in a demanding world, all of us have mountains to climb and mountains to move. Moving those mountains requires faith.

Are you a mountain-mover whose faith is evident for all to see? Or, are you a spiritual underachiever? As you think about the answer to that question, consider this: God needs more people who are willing to move mountains for His glory and for His kingdom.

Every life—including yours—is a series of wins and losses. Every step of the way, through every triumph and tragedy, God walks with you, ready and willing to strengthen you. So the next time you find your courage tested to the limit, remember to take your fears to God. If you call upon Him, you will be comforted. Whatever your challenge, whatever your trouble, God can handle it.

When you place your faith, your trust, indeed your life in the hands of your Heavenly Father, you'll be amazed at the marvelous things He can do with you and through you. So strengthen your faith through praise, through worship, through Bible study, and through prayer. And trust God's plans. With Him, all things are possible, and He stands ready to open a world of possibilities to you . . . if you have faith.

And now, with no more delays, let the mountain moving begin.

Faith should be practiced more than studied. Vance Havner said, "Nothing is more disastrous than to study faith, analyze faith, make noble resolves of faith, but never actually to make the leap of faith." How true!

I am truly grateful that faith enables me to move past the question of "Why?"

Zig Ziglar

Faith is trusting in advance what will only make sense in reverse.

Phillip Yancey

Faith in faith is pointless. Faith in a living, active God moves mountains.

Beth Moore

Let me encourage you to continue to wait with faith. God may not perform a miracle, but He is trustworthy to touch you and make you whole where there used to be a hole.

Lisa Whelchel

Faith is the willingness to receive whatever he wants to give, or the willingness not to have what he does not want to give.

Elisabeth Elliot

More from God's Word about Faith

Now faith is the reality of what is hoped for, the proof of what is not seen.

Hebrews 11:1 HCSB

For we walk by faith, not by sight.

2 Corinthians 5:7 HCSB

If you do not stand firm in your faith, then you will not stand at all.

Isaiah 7:9 HCSB

 ## Notes to Yourself about the Power of Faith

_____

_____

_____

_____

_____

_____

_____

82

CHAPTER 18

THE IMPORTANCE OF WORSHIP

But an hour is coming, and is now here, when the true worshipers will worship the Father in spirit and truth. Yes, the Father wants such people to worship Him. God is Spirit, and those who worship Him must worship in spirit and truth.

John 4:23-24 HCSB

Here's a simple question: Why do you attend church? Is it because of your sincere desire to worship and to praise God? Hopefully you can honestly answer yes. Yet far too many Christians attend worship services because they believe they are "supposed to go to church" or because they feel "pressured" to attend. Still others go to church for "social" reasons. But make no mistake: the best reason to attend church is out of a sincere desire to please God, to praise God, to experience God, and to discern God's will for your life.

Some people may tell you that they don't engage in worship. Don't believe them. All of mankind is engaged in worship. The question is not whether we worship, but what we worship. Wise people choose to worship God. When they do, they are blessed with a plentiful harvest of joy, peace, and abundance. Other people choose to distance themselves from God by foolishly worshiping things that are intended to bring personal gratification but not spiritual gratification. Such choices often have tragic consequences.

How can we ensure that we cast our lot with God? We do so, in part, by the practice of regular, purposeful worship in the company of fellow believers. When we worship God faithfully and fervently, we are blessed. When we fail to worship God, for whatever reason, we forfeit the spiritual gifts that might otherwise be ours.

We must worship our heavenly Father, not just with our words, but also with deeds. We must honor Him, praise Him, and obey Him. As we seek to find purpose and meaning for our lives, we must first seek His purpose and His will. For believers, God comes first. Always first.

The best way to worship God . . . is to worship Him sincerely and often.

The most common mistake Christians make in worship today is seeking an experience rather than seeking God.

Rick Warren

It's our privilege to not only raise our hands in worship but also to combine the visible with the invisible in a rising stream of praise and adoration sent directly to our Father.

Shirley Dobson

Each time, before you intercede, be quiet first and worship God in His glory. Think of what He can do and how He delights to hear the prayers of His redeemed people. Think of your place and privilege in Christ, and expect great things!

Andrew Murray

Spiritual worship comes from our very core and is fueled by an awesome reverence and desire for God.

Beth Moore

It is impossible to worship God and remain unchanged.

Henry Blackaby

More from God's Word about Worship

So that at the name of Jesus every knee should bow—of those who are in heaven and on earth and under the earth—and every tongue should confess that Jesus Christ is Lord, to the glory of God the Father.

Philippians 2:10-11 HCSB

Worship the Lord your God and . . . serve Him only.

Matthew 4:10 HCSB

If anyone is thirsty, he should come to Me and drink!

John 7:37 HCSB

Notes to Yourself about the Importance of Worship

_____

_____

_____

_____

_____

_____

CHAPTER 19

KEEPING THINGS IN PROPER PERSPECTIVE

How much better to get wisdom than gold, to choose understanding rather than silver!

Proverbs 16:16 NIV

For most of us, life is busy and complicated. Amid the rush and crush of the daily grind, it is easy to lose perspective . . . easy, but wrong. When our world seems to be spinning out of control, we can regain perspective by slowing ourselves down and then turning our thoughts and prayers toward God.

Do you carve out quiet moments each day to offer thanksgiving and praise to your Creator? You should. During these moments of stillness, you will often sense the love and wisdom of our Lord.

The familiar words of Psalm 46:10 remind us to "Be still, and know that I am God" (NKJV). When we do so, we encounter the awesome presence of our loving Heavenly Father, and we are blessed beyond words. But, when we ignore the presence of our Creator, we rob ourselves of His perspective, His peace, and His joy.

Today and every day, make time to be still before God. When you do, you can face the day's complications with the wisdom and power that only He can provide.

Keep life in perspective: Your life is an integral part of God's grand plan. So don't become unduly upset over the minor inconveniences of life, and don't worry too much about today's setbacks—they're temporary.

Earthly fears are no fears at all. Answer the big question of eternity, and the little questions of life fall into perspective.

Max Lucado

The Bible is a remarkable commentary on perspective. Through its divine message, we are brought face to face with issues and tests in daily living and how, by the power of the Holy Spirit, we are enabled to respond positively to them.

Luci Swindoll

Joy is the direct result of having God's perspective on our daily lives and the effect of loving our Lord enough to obey His commands and trust His promises.

Bill Bright

Instead of being frustrated and overwhelmed by all that is going on in our world, go to the Lord and ask Him to give you His eternal perspective.

Kay Arthur

Like a shadow declining swiftly . . . away . . . like the dew of the morning gone with the heat of the day; like the wind in the treetops, like a wave of the sea, so are our lives on earth when seen in light of eternity.

Ruth Bell Graham

More from God's Word about Perspective

If you need wisdom—if you want to know what God wants you to do—ask him, and he will gladly tell you. He will not resent your asking.

James 1:5 NLT

For now we see in a mirror, dimly, but then face to face. Now I know in part, but then I shall know just as I also am known.

1 Corinthians 13:12 NKJV

To acquire wisdom is to love oneself; people who cherish understanding will prosper.

Proverbs 19:8 NLT

Notes to Yourself about the Importance of Maintaining Perspective

_____

_____

_____

_____

_____

CHAPTER 20

WHEN IT NEEDS TO BE DONE, DO IT!

Therefore, get your minds ready for action, being self-disciplined, and set your hope completely on the grace to be brought to you at the revelation of Jesus Christ.

1 Peter 1:13 HCSB

Here's a rule for your journey that's worth remembering: When something important needs to be done, the best time to do it is sooner rather than later. But sometimes, instead of doing the smart thing (which, by the way, is choosing "sooner"), you may choose "later." When you do, you may pay a heavy price.

The habit of procrastination takes a two-fold toll on its victims. First, important work goes unfinished; second (and more importantly), valuable energy is wasted in the process of putting off the things that remain undone. Procrastination results from an individual's short-sighted attempt to postpone temporary discomfort. What results is a sense-less cycle of (1) Delay, followed by (2) Worry followed by

(3) A panicky and futile attempt to "catch up." Procrastination is, at its core, a struggle against oneself; the only antidote is action.

Once you acquire the habit of doing what needs to be done when it needs to be done, you will avoid untold trouble, worry, and stress. So learn to defeat procrastination by paying less attention to your fears and more attention to your responsibilities.

Are you one of those people who puts things off till the last minute? If so, it's time to change your ways. Whatever "it" is, do it now. When you do, you won't have to worry about "it" later.

It's easy to put off unpleasant tasks until "later." A far better strategy is this: Do the unpleasant work first so you can enjoy the rest of the day.

Not now becomes never.

Martin Luther

Now is the only time worth having because, indeed, it is the only time we have.

C. H. Spurgeon

Do noble things, do not dream them all day long.

Charles Kingsley

Every time you refuse to face up to life and its problems, you weaken your character.

E. Stanley Jones

I've found that the worst thing I can do when it comes to any kind of potential pressure situation is to put off dealing with it.

John Maxwell

I cannot fix what I will not face.

Jim Gallery

More from God's Word about Procrastination

When you make a vow to God, don't delay fulfilling it, because He does not delight in fools. Fulfill what you vow.

Ecclesiastes 5:4 HCSB

Whatever you do, do it enthusiastically, as something done for the Lord and not for men.

Colossians 3:23 HCSB

If you falter in times of trouble, how small is your strength!

Proverbs 24:10 NIV

Notes to Yourself about the Importance of Defeating Procrastination

_____

_____

_____

_____

_____

_____

CHAPTER 21

THE COMPANY YOU KEEP

He who walks with wise men will be wise, but the companion of fools will be destroyed.

Proverbs 13:20 NKJV

Are you a people-pleaser or a God-pleaser? Hopefully, you're far more concerned with pleasing God than you are with pleasing your friends. But even if you're a devoted Christian, you may, from time to time, feel the urge to impress your friends and acquaintances—and sometimes that urge will be strong.

Peer pressure can be good or bad, depending upon who your peers are and how they behave. If your friends encourage you to follow God's will and to obey His commandments, then you'll experience positive peer pressure, and that's a good thing. But, if your friends encourage you to do foolish things, then you're facing a different kind of peer pressure . . . and you'd better beware. When you feel pressured to do things—or to say things—that lead you away from God, you're heading straight for trouble. So don't do the "easy" thing or the "popular" thing. Do the right thing, and don't worry about winning any popularity contests.

Are you satisfied to follow the crowd? If so, you will probably pay a heavy price for your shortsightedness. But if you're determined to follow the One from Galilee, He will guide your steps and bless your undertakings. To sum it up, here's your choice: you can choose to please God first, or you can fall prey to peer pressure. The choice is yours—and so are the consequences.

Put peer pressure to work for you. How? By associating with people who, by their actions and their words, will encourage you to become a better person.

You will get untold flak for prioritizing God's revealed and present will for your life over man's . . . but, boy, is it worth it.

Beth Moore

Do you want to be wise? Choose wise friends.

Charles Swindoll

For better or worse, you will eventually become more and more like the people you associate with. So why not associate with people who make you better, not worse?

Marie T. Freeman

It is comfortable to know that we are responsible to God and not to man. It is a small matter to be judged of man's judgement.

Lottie Moon

I have found that the closer I am to the godly people around me, the easier it is for me to live a righteous life because they hold me accountable.

John MacArthur

More from God's Word about Peer Pressure

Am I now trying to win the approval of men, or of God?

Galatians 1:10 NIV

Stay away from a foolish man, for you will not find knowledge on his lips.

Proverbs 14:7 NIV

My son, if sinners entice you, do not consent.

Proverbs 1:10 NKJV

Notes to Yourself about the Power of Peer Pressure

_____

_____

_____

_____

_____

_____

_____

CHAPTER 22

TREAT YOUR BODY WITH CARE

Therefore, I urge you, brothers, in view of God's mercy, to offer your bodies as living sacrifices, holy and pleasing to God—this is your spiritual act of worship.

Romans 12:1 NIV

How do you treat your body? Do you treat it with the reverence and respect it deserves, or do you take it more or less for granted? Well, the Bible has clear instructions about the way you should take care of the miraculous body that God has given you.

God's Word teaches us that our bodies are "temples" in which belong to God (1 Corinthians 6:19-20). We are commanded (not encouraged, not advised—we are commanded!) to treat our bodies with respect and honor. We do so by making wise choices and by making those choices consistently over an extended period of time.

Do you sincerely seek to improve the overall quality of your life and your health? Then promise yourself—and God—that you will begin making the kind of wise choices that will lead to a longer, healthier, happier life. The responsibility for those choices is yours. And so are the rewards.

God's Word is full of advice about health, moderation, and sensible living. When you come across these passages, take them to heart and put them to use.

God wants you to give Him your body.
Some people do foolish things with their bodies.
God wants your body as a holy sacrifice.

—

Warren Wiersbe

Whenever I read the words of Isaiah that say those who "wait on the Lord" shall "run and not be weary" and "walk and not faint," I'm reminded of how naturally spiritual development and endurance exercise go together.

Dr. Kenneth Cooper

If you desire to improve your physical well-being and your emotional outlook, increasing your faith can help you.

John Maxwell

Laughter is the language of the young at heart and the antidote to what ails us.

Barbara Johnson

You can't buy good health at the doctor's office—you've got to earn it for yourself.

Marie T. Freeman

Birds which are too heavy cannot fly very high. The same is true of those who mistreat their bodies.

St. John Climacus

More from God's Word about Fitness

Don't you know that you are God's sanctuary and that the Spirit of God lives in you?

1 Corinthians 3:16 HCSB

For we know that if our earthly house, a tent, is destroyed, we have a building from God, a house not made with hands, eternal in the heavens.

2 Corinthians 5:1 HCSB

For it was You who created my inward parts; You knit me together in my mother's womb. I will praise You, because I have been remarkably and wonderfully made.

Psalm 139:13-14 HCSB

 Notes to Yourself about the Rewards of Staying Fit

CHAPTER 23

A WILLINGNESS
TO SERVE

*So think clearly and exercise self-control. Look forward to the
special blessings that will come to you at the return of Jesus Christ.*

1 Peter 1:13 NLT

We live in a world that glorifies power, prestige, fame,
and money. But the words of Jesus teach us that the
most esteemed men and women in this world are not the self-
congratulatory leaders of society but are instead the humblest
of servants.

Are you willing to become a humble servant for Christ?
Are you willing to pitch in and make the world a better place,
or are you determined to keep all your blessings to yourself.
The answers to these questions will determine the quantity
and the quality of the service you render to God and to His
children.

Today, you may feel the temptation to take more than
you give. You may be tempted to withhold your generosity.
Or you may be tempted to build yourself up in the eyes of
your friends. Resist those temptations. Instead, serve your

friends quietly and without fanfare. Find a need and fill it . . . humbly. Lend a helping hand . . . anonymously. Share a word of kindness . . . with quiet sincerity. As you go about your daily activities, remember that the Savior of all humanity made Himself a servant, and we, as His followers, must do no less.

Whatever your age, whatever your circumstances, you can serve: Each stage of life's journey is a glorious opportunity to place yourself in the service of the One who is the Giver of all blessings. As long as you live, you should honor God with your service to others.

Service is the pathway to real significance.

Rick Warren

God wants us to serve Him with a willing spirit, one that would choose no other way.

Beth Moore

Christianity, in its purest form, is nothing more than seeing Jesus. Christian service, in its purest form, is nothing more than imitating him who we see. To see his Majesty and to imitate him: that is the sum of Christianity.

Max Lucado

God has lots of folks who intend to go to work for him "some day." What He needs is more people who are willing to work for Him today.

Marie T. Freeman

We do the works, but God works in us in the doing of the works.

St. Augustine

More from God's Word about Service

Worship the Lord your God and . . . serve Him only.

Matthew 4:10 HCSB

A person should consider us in this way: as servants of Christ and managers of God's mysteries. In this regard, it is expected of managers that each one be found faithful.

1 Corinthians 4:1-2 HCSB

If they obey and serve him, they will spend the rest of their days in prosperity and their years in contentment.

Job 36:11 NIV

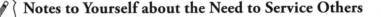 **Notes to Yourself about the Need to Service Others**

_____

_____

_____

_____

_____

_____

CHAPTER 24

LIVING COURAGEOUSLY

Be strong and of good courage, and do it; do not fear nor be dismayed, for the Lord God—my God—will be with you. He will not leave you nor forsake you, until you have finished all the work for the service of the house of the Lord.

1 Chronicles 28:20 NKJV

A storm rose quickly on the Sea of Galilee, and the disciples were afraid. Although they had seen Jesus perform many miracles, although they had walked side by side with the Son of God, the disciples feared for their lives. So they turned to their Savior, and He calmed the waters and the wind.

Sometimes, we, like the disciples, feel threatened by the inevitable storms of life. When we are fearful, we, too, can turn to Christ for courage and for comfort. When we do so, He calms our fears just as surely as He calmed the winds and the waters two thousand years ago.

Billy Graham observed, "Down through the centuries, in times of trouble and trial, God has brought courage to the hearts of those who love Him. The Bible is filled with assurances of God's help and comfort in every kind of trouble which might cause fears to arise in the human heart. You can look ahead with promise, hope, and joy."

The next time you find your courage tested by the inevitable challenges of everyday living, remember that God is as near as your next breath. He is your shield and your strength; He is your protector and your deliverer. Call upon Him in your hour of need and then be comforted. Whatever your challenge, whatever your trouble, God can handle it. And will.

Is your courage being tested? Cling tightly to God's promises, and pray. God can give you the strength to meet any challenge, and that's exactly what you should ask Him to do.

With each new experience of letting God be in control, we gain courage and reinforcement for daring to do it again and again.

Gloria Gaither

There comes a time when we simply have to face the challenges in our lives and stop backing down.

John Eldredge

The truth of Christ brings assurance and so removes the former problem of fear and uncertainty.

A. W. Tozer

What is courage? It is the ability to be strong in trust, in conviction, in obedience. To be courageous is to step out in faith—to trust and obey, no matter what.

Kay Arthur

God knows that the strength that comes from wrestling with our fear will give us wings to fly.

Paula Rinehart

More from God's Word about Courage

But when Jesus heard it, He answered him, "Don't be afraid. Only believe."

Luke 8:50 HCSB

For God has not given us a spirit of fearfulness, but one of power, love, and sound judgment.

2 Timothy 1:7 HCSB

Be on guard. Stand true to what you believe. Be courageous. Be strong.

1 Corinthians 16:13 NLT

 ### Notes to Yourself about the Need for Courage

CHAPTER 25

GOD'S PERFECT LOVE

*And we have known and believed the love that God has for us.
God is love, and he who abides in love abides in God, and God
in him.*

1 John 4:16 NKJV

God's love for you is bigger and better than you can imagine. In fact, God's love is far too big to comprehend (in this lifetime). But this much we know: God loves you so much that He sent His Son Jesus to come to this earth and to die for you. And, when you accepted Jesus into your heart, God gave you a gift that is more precious than gold: the gift of eternal life. Now, precisely because you are a wondrous creation treasured by God, a question presents itself: What will you do in response to God's love? Will you ignore it or embrace it? Will you return it or neglect it? The decision, of course, is yours and yours alone.

When you embrace God's love, you are forever changed. When you embrace God's love, you feel differently about yourself, your neighbors, and your world. When you embrace God's love, you share His message and you obey His commandments.

When you accept the Father's gift of grace, you are blessed here on earth and throughout all eternity. So do yourself a favor right now: accept God's love with open arms and welcome His Son Jesus into your heart. When you do, your life will be changed today, tomorrow, and forever.

God's love for you is too big to understand with your brain . . . but it's not too big to feel with your heart.

If God had a refrigerator, your picture would be on it. If he had a wallet, your photo would be in it. He sends you flowers every spring and a sunrise every morning.

Max Lucado

God loves each of us as if there were only one of us.

St. Augustine

Joy comes from knowing God loves me and knows who I am and where I'm going . . . that my future is secure as I rest in Him.

James Dobson

The hope we have in Jesus is the anchor for the soul—something sure and steadfast, preventing drifting or giving way, lowered to the depth of God's love.

Franklin Graham

God will never let you be shaken or moved from your place near His heart.

Joni Eareckson Tada

More from God's Word about God's Love

For God so loved the world, that he gave his only begotten Son, that whosoever believeth in him should not perish, but have everlasting life.

John 3:16 KJV

For the Lord is good, and His love is eternal; His faithfulness endures through all generations.

Psalm 100:5 HCSB

Help me, Lord my God; save me according to Your faithful love.

Psalm 109:26 HCSB

Notes to Yourself about God's Love

CHAPTER 26

FOLLOWING CHRIST

And he said to them all, If any man will come after me, let him deny himself, and take up his cross daily, and follow me. For whosoever will save his life shall lose it: but whosoever will lose his life for my sake, the same shall save it.

Luke 9:23-24 KJV

Who are you going to walk with today? Are you going to walk with people who worship the ways of the world? Or are you going to walk with the Son of God? Jesus walks with you. Are you walking with Him? Hopefully, you will choose to walk with Him today and every day of your life.

Jesus loved you so much that He endured unspeakable humiliation and suffering for you. How will you respond to Christ's sacrifice? Will you take up His cross and follow Him (Luke 9:23), or will you choose another path? When you place your hopes squarely at the foot of the cross, when you place Jesus squarely at the center of your life, you will be blessed.

The 19th-century writer Hannah Whitall Smith observed, "The crucial question for each of us is this: What do you think of Jesus, and do you yet have a personal acquaintance with Him?" Indeed, the answer to that question determines the quality, the course, and the direction of our lives today and for all eternity.

Today provides another glorious opportunity to place yourself in the service of the One from Galilee. May you seek His will, may you trust His word, and may you walk in His footsteps—now and forever—amen.

If you want to be a little more like Christ . . . learn about His teachings, follow in His footsteps, and obey His commandments.

Walk in the daylight of God's will because then you will be safe; you will not stumble.

Anne Graham Lotz

When we truly walk with God throughout our day, life slowly starts to fall into place.

Bill Hybels

Think of this—we may live together with Him here and now, a daily walking with Him who loved us and gave Himself for us.

Elisabeth Elliot

A disciple is a follower of Christ. That means you take on His priorities as your own. His agenda becomes your agenda. His mission becomes your mission.

Charles Stanley

Imagine the spiritual strength the disciples drew from walking hundreds of miles with Jesus . . . 3 John 4.

John Maxwell

More from God's Word about Following Christ

But whoever keeps His word, truly in him the love of God is perfected. This is how we know we are in Him: the one who says he remains in Him should walk just as He walked.

1 John 2:5-6 HCSB

We encouraged, comforted, and implored each one of you to walk worthy of God, who calls you into His own kingdom and glory.

1 Thessalonians 2:12 HCSB

I urge you to live a life worthy of the calling you have received.

Ephesians 4:1 NIV

 ## Notes to Yourself about Following Christ

_____

_____

_____

_____

_____

_____

CHAPTER 27

THE POWER OF ENCOURAGEMENT

So encourage each other and give each other strength, just as you are doing now.

1 Thessalonians 5:11 NCV

Life is a team sport, and all of us need occasional pats on the back from our teammates. This world can be a difficult place, a place where many of our friends and family members are troubled by the challenges of everyday life. And since we cannot always be certain who needs our help, we should strive to speak helpful words to all who cross our paths.

Genuine encouragement should never be confused with pity. God intends for His children to lead lives of abundance, joy, celebration and praise—not lives of self-pity or regret. So we must guard ourselves against hosting (or joining) the "pity parties" that so often accompany difficult times. Instead, we must encourage each other to have faith—first in God and His only begotten Son—and then in our own abilities to use the talents God has given us for the furtherance of His kingdom and for the betterment of our own lives.

As a faithful follower of Jesus, you have every reason to be hopeful, and you have every reason to share your hopes with others. When you do, you will discover that hope, like other human emotions, is contagious. So do the world (and yourself) a favor: Look for the good in others and celebrate the good that you find. When you do, you'll be a powerful force of encouragement to your friends and family . . . and a worthy servant to your God.

Sometimes, even a very few words can make a very big difference. As Fanny Crosby observed, "A single word, if spoken in a friendly spirit, may be sufficient to turn one from dangerous error."

Words. Do you fully understand their power? Can any of us really grasp the mighty force behind the things we say? Do we stop and think before we speak, considering the potency of the words we utter?

Joni Eareckson Tada

One of the ways God refills us after failure is through the blessing of Christian fellowship. Just experiencing the joy of simple activities shared with other children of God can have a healing effect on us.

Anne Graham Lotz

We urgently need people who encourage and inspire us to move toward God and away from the world's enticing pleasures.

Jim Cymbala

Discouraged people don't need critics. They hurt enough already. They don't need more guilt or piled-on distress. They need encouragement. They need a refuge, a willing, caring, available someone.

Charles Swindoll

More from God's Word about Encouragement

I want their hearts to be encouraged and joined together in love, so that they may have all the riches of assured understanding, and have the knowledge of God's mystery—Christ.

Colossians 2:2 HCSB

Bear one another's burdens, and so fulfill the law of Christ.

Galatians 6:2 NKJV

You must warn each other every day, as long as it is called "today," so that none of you will be deceived by sin and hardened against God.

Hebrews 3:13 NLT

Notes to Yourself about the Power of Encouragement

CHAPTER 28

PROBLEM-SOLVING 101

God is our refuge and strength, a very present help in trouble.

Psalm 46:1 NKJV

Here's a riddle: What is it that is too unimportant to pray about yet too big for God to handle? The answer, of course, is: "nothing." Yet sometimes, when the challenges of the day seem overwhelming, we may spend more time worrying about our troubles than praying about them. And, we may spend more time fretting about our problems than solving them. A far better strategy, of course, is to pray as if everything depended entirely upon God and to work as if everything depended entirely upon us.

Life is an exercise in problem-solving. The question is not whether we will encounter problems; the real question is how we will choose to address them. When it comes to solving the problems of everyday living, we often know precisely what needs to be done, but we may be slow in doing it—especially if what needs to be done is difficult or uncomfortable for us. So we put off till tomorrow what should be done today.

The words of Psalm 34 remind us that the Lord solves problems for "people who do what is right." And usually, "doing what is right" means doing the uncomfortable work of confronting our problems sooner rather than later. So with no further ado, let the problem-solving begin . . . now!

Every problem comes gift-wrapped in a package that also contains a creative solution. When you open the package that contains the problem, the solution is there, too. Your job is to accept both gifts.

Press on. Obstacles are seldom
the same size tomorrow as they are today.

—

Robert Schuller

You've got problems; I've got problems; all God's children have got problems. The question is how are you going to deal with them?

John Maxwell

Faith does not eliminate problems. Faith keeps you in a trusting relationship with God in the midst of your problems.

Henry Blackaby

The happiest people in the world are not those who have no problems, but the people who have learned to live with those things that are less than perfect.

James Dobson

Life will be made or broken at the place where we meet and deal with obstacles.

E. Stanley Jones

Whoever you are, whatever your condition or circumstance, whatever your past or problem, Jesus can restore you to wholeness.

Anne Graham Lotz

More from God's Word about Problems

I will be with you when you pass through the waters . . . when you walk through the fire . . . the flame will not burn you. For I the Lord your God, the Holy One of Israel, and your Savior.

Isaiah 43:2-3 HCSB

Then they cried out to the Lord in their trouble, and He saved them out of their distresses.

Psalm 107:13 NKJV

If you do nothing in a difficult time, your strength is limited.

Proverbs 24:10 HCSB

 Notes to Yourself about Your Biggest Problem (and the Way You Can Solve It)

_____

_____

_____

_____

_____

CHAPTER 29

TACKLING TOUGH TIMES

We also rejoice in our afflictions, because we know that affliction produces endurance, endurance produces proven character, and proven character produces hope.

Romans 5:3-4 HCSB

The Bible promises this: tough times are temporary but God's love is not—God's love lasts forever. So what does that mean to you? Just this: From time to time, everybody faces tough times, and so will you. And when tough times arrive, God will always stand ready to protect you and heal you.

Psalm 147 promises, "He heals the brokenhearted" (v. 3, NIV), but Psalm 147 doesn't say that He heals them instantly. Usually, it takes time (and maybe even a little help from you) for God to fix things. So if you're facing tough times, face them with God by your side. If you find yourself in any kind of trouble, pray about it and ask God for help. And be patient. God will work things out, just as He has promised, but He will do it in His own way and in His own time.

As believers, we know that God loves us and that He will protect us. In times of hardship, He will comfort us; in times of sorrow, He will dry our tears. When we are troubled, or weak, or sorrowful, God is always with us. We must build our lives on the rock that cannot be shaken: we must trust in God. And then, we must get on with the hard work of tackling our problems . . . because if we don't, who will? Or should?

Going through tough times? Maybe there's a lesson in there somewhere. If you're going through difficult times, consider it an opportunity for spiritual growth. And ask yourself this question: "What is God trying to teach me today?"

When you accept the fact that sometimes seasons are dry and times are hard and that God is in control of both, you will discover a sense of divine refuge because the hope then is in God and not in yourself.

Charles Swindoll

When God allows extraordinary trials for His people, He prepares extraordinary comforts for them.

Corrie ten Boom

We can stand affliction better than we can stand prosperity, for in prosperity we forget God.

D. L. Moody

Life will be made or broken at the place where we meet and deal with obstacles.

E. Stanley Jones

Don't let circumstances distress you. Rather, look for the will of God for your life to be revealed in and through those circumstances.

Billy Graham

More from God's Word about Adversity

The LORD also will be a stronghold for the oppressed, a stronghold in times of trouble.

Psalm 9:9 NASB

We are pressured in every way but not crushed; we are perplexed but not in despair.

2 Corinthians 4:8 HCSB

I called to the Lord in my distress; I called to my God. From His temple He heard my voice.

2 Samuel 22:7 HCSB

 Notes to Yourself about Overcoming Tough Times

CHAPTER 30

STEWARDSHIP OF YOUR TIME

So teach us to number our days, that we may gain a heart of wisdom.

Psalm 90:12 NKJV

Time is a nonrenewable gift from God. But sometimes, we treat our time here on earth as if it were not a gift at all: We may be tempted to invest our lives in trivial pursuits and mindless diversions. But our Father in heaven wants us to do more . . . much more.

Are you one of those people who puts things off until the last minute? Do you waste time doing things that don't matter very much while putting off the important things until it's too late to do the job right? If so, it's now time to start making better choices.

As you establish priorities for your day and your life, remember that each new day is a special treasure to be savored and celebrated. As a Christian, you have much to celebrate and much to do. It's up to you, and you alone, to honor God for the gift of time by using that gift wisely. Every day, like every life, is composed of moments. Each moment of your life holds within it the potential to seek God's will and to serve His purposes. If you are wise, you will strive to do both.

It may seem like you've got all the time in the world to do the things you need to do, but time is shorter than you think. Time here on earth is limited . . . use it or lose it!

Finding time for God takes time . . . and it's up to you to find it. The world is constantly vying for your attention, and sometimes the noise can be deafening. Remember the words of Elisabeth Elliot; she said, "The world is full of noise. Let us learn the art of silence, stillness, and solitude."

Our time is short! The time we can invest for God, in creative things, in receiving our fellowmen for Christ, is short!

Billy Graham

As we surrender the use of our time to the lordship of Christ, He will lead us to use it in the most productive way imaginable.

Charles Stanley

Overcommitment and time pressures are the greatest destroyers of marriages and families. It takes time to develop any friendship, whether with a loved one or with God himself.

James Dobson

Life's unfolding stops for no one.

Kathy Troccoli

God has a present will for your life. It is neither chaotic nor utterly exhausting. In the midst of many good choices vying for your time, He will give you the discernment to recognize what is best.

Beth Moore

More from God's Word about Time Management

When you make a vow to God, don't delay fulfilling it, because He does not delight in fools. Fulfill what you vow.

Ecclesiastes 5:4 HCSB

If you falter in times of trouble, how small is your strength!

Proverbs 24:10 NIV

But be doers of the word, and not hearers only, deceiving yourselves.

James 1:22 NKJV

 ## Notes to Yourself about Time Management

_____

_____

_____

_____

_____

_____

_____

CHAPTER 31

THE POWER OF SIMPLICITY

"You've gotten a reputation as a bad-news people, you people of Judah and Israel, but I'm coming to save you. From now on, you're the good-news people. Don't be afraid. Keep a firm grip on what I'm doing." Keep Your Lives Simple and Honest.

Zechariah 8:13 MSG

You live in a world where simplicity is in short supply. Certainly, you are the beneficiary of many technological innovations, but these innovations have a price: in all likelihood, your world is highly complex. From the moment you wake up in the morning until the time you lay your head on the pillow at night, you are the target of an endless stream of audio and video. Many of these messages are intended to grab your attention in order to convince you to purchase things you didn't know you needed (and probably don't!). To make matters worse, many aspects of your life, including big stuff like education and health care, are caught in the undertow of an ever-increasing flood of government rules and regulations. So unless you take firm control of your time and your life, you may be overwhelmed by a tidal wave of red tape accompanied by a flood of distractions.

Is yours a life of moderation or accumulation? Are you more interested in the possessions you can acquire or in the person you can become? The answers to these questions will determine the direction of your day and, in time, the direction of your life.

If your material possessions are somehow distancing you from God, get rid of them. If your outside interests leave you too little time for your family or your faith, slow down the merry-go-round, or better yet, get off the merry-go-round completely. Remember: God wants your full attention, and He wants it today, so don't let anybody or anything get in His way.

Give simplicity a try now: Perhaps you think that the more stuff you acquire, the happier you'll be. If so, think again. Too much stuff means too many headaches, so start simplifying now.

The most powerful life is the most simple life. The most powerful life is the life that knows where it's going, that knows where the source of strength is; it is the life that stays free of clutter and happenstance and hurriedness.

Max Lucado

Efficiency is enhanced not by what we accomplish but more often by what we relinquish.

Charles Swindoll

Nobody is going to simplify your life for you. You've got to simplify things for yourself.

Marie T. Freeman

There is absolutely no evidence that complexity and materialism lead to happiness. On the contrary, there is plenty of evidence that simplicity and spirituality lead to joy, a blessedness that is better than happiness.

Dennis Swanberg

He is rich that is satisfied.

Thomas Fuller

More from God's Word about Simplicity

A simple life in the Fear-of-God is better than a rich life with a ton of headaches.

Proverbs 15:16 MSG

We brought nothing into the world, so we can take nothing out. But, if we have food and clothes, we will be satisfied with that.

1 Timothy 6:7-8 NCV

Do not love the world or the things in the world. If anyone loves the world, the love of the Father is not in him.

1 John 2:15 NKJV

 ## Notes to Yourself about the Value of Simplicity

CHAPTER 32

DON'T WORRY

So do not worry, saying, "What shall we eat?" or "What shall we drink?" or "What shall we wear?" For the pagans run after all these things, and your heavenly Father knows that you need them. But seek first his kingdom and his righteousness, and all these things will be given to you as well. Therefore do not worry about tomorrow, for tomorrow will worry about itself. Each day has enough trouble of its own.

Matthew 6:31-34 NIV

Because you have the ability to think, you also have the ability to worry. Even if you're a very faithful Christian, you may be plagued by occasional periods of discouragement and doubt. Even though you trust God's promise of salvation—even though you sincerely believe in God's love and protection—you may find yourself upset by the countless details of everyday life. When you're worried, there are two places you should take your concerns: to the people who love you and to God.

When troubles arise, it helps to talk about them with parents, concerned adults, and trusted friends. But you shouldn't stop there: you should also talk to God through your prayers.

If you're worried about something, pray about it. Remember that God is always listening, and He always wants to hear from you.

So when you're upset about something, try this simple plan: talk and pray. Talk openly to the people who love you, and pray to the Heavenly Father who made you. The more you talk and the more you pray, the better you'll feel.

When you're having hard times, remember that this, too, will pass. And remember that it will pass more quickly if you spend more time solving problems and less time fretting over them.

With the peace of God to guard us and the God of peace to guide us—why worry?

Warren Wiersbe

The closer you live to God, the smaller everything else appears.

Rick Warren

Never yield to gloomy anticipation. Place your hope and confidence in God. He has no record of failure.

Mrs. Charles E. Cowman

Worry makes you forget who's in charge.

Max Lucado

Since the Lord is your shepherd, what are you worried about?

Marie T. Freeman

Submit each day to God, knowing that He is God over all your tomorrows.

Kay Arthur

More from God's Word about Worry

Be anxious for nothing, but in everything by prayer and supplication with thanksgiving let your requests be made known to God.

Philippians 4:6 NASB

When you pass through the waters, I will be with you; and through the rivers, they shall not overflow you. When you walk through the fire, you shall not be burned, nor shall the flame scorch you. For I am the Lord your God, The Holy One of Israel, your Savior.

Isaiah 43:2-3 NKJV

Those who trust in the Lord are like Mount Zion. It cannot be shaken; it remains forever.

Psalm 125:1 HCSB

Notes to Yourself about Defeating Worry

_____

_____

_____

_____

_____

CHAPTER 33

THE POWER OF PERSEVERANCE

Do you not know that those who run in a race all run, but one receives the prize? Run in such a way that you may obtain it. And everyone who competes for the prize is temperate in all things. Now they do it to obtain a perishable crown, but we for an imperishable crown.

1 Corinthians 9:24-25 NKJV

As you travel life's path, you will undoubtedly experience your fair share of disappointments, detours, false starts, and failures. When you do, don't become discouraged: God's not finished with you yet.

The old saying is as true today as it was when it was first spoken: "Life is a marathon, not a sprint." That's why wise travelers (like you) select a traveling companion who never tires and never falters. That partner, of course, is your Heavenly Father.

The next time you find your courage tested to the limit, remember that God is as near as your next breath, and remember that He offers strength and comfort to His children.

He is your shield and your strength; He is your protector and your deliverer. Call upon Him in your hour of need and then be comforted. Whatever your challenge, whatever your trouble, God can help you persevere. And that's precisely what He'll do if you ask Him.

Perhaps you are in a hurry for God to help you resolve your difficulties. Perhaps you're anxious to earn the rewards that you feel you've already earned from life. Perhaps you're drumming your fingers, impatiently waiting for God to act. If so, be forewarned: God operates on His own timetable, not yours. Sometimes, God may answer your prayers with silence, and when He does, you must patiently persevere. In times of trouble, you must remain steadfast and trust in the merciful goodness of your Heavenly Father. Whatever your problem, He can handle it. Your job is to keep persevering until He does.

Life is difficult and success requires effort—so perseverance pays big dividends.

In the Bible, patience is not a passive acceptance of circumstances. It is a courageous perseverance in the face of suffering and difficulty.

Warren Wiersbe

Love is a steady wish for the loved person's ultimate good.

C. S. Lewis

Battles are won in the trenches, in the grit and grime of courageous determination; they are won day by day in the arena of life.

Charles Swindoll

Failure is one of life's most powerful teachers. How we handle our failures determines whether we're going to simply "get by" in life or "press on."

Beth Moore

Jesus taught that perseverance is the essential element in prayer.

E. M. Bounds

More from God's Word about Perseverance

But as for you, be strong; don't be discouraged, for your work has a reward.

2 Chronicles 15:7 HCSB

I have fought the good fight, I have finished the race, I have kept the faith.

2 Timothy 4:7 HCSB

Be strong and courageous, and do the work.

1 Chronicles 28:20 HCSB

Notes to Yourself about the Power of Perseverance

CHAPTER 34

BEWARE OF PERFECTIONISM

Those who wait for perfect weather will never plant seeds; those who look at every cloud will never harvest crops. . . . Plant early in the morning, and work until evening, because you don't know if this or that will succeed. They might both do well.

Ecclesiastes 11:4,6 NCV

You live in a world where expectations are high, incredibly high, or unreachable. The media delivers an endless stream of messages that tell you how to look, how to behave, how to eat, and how to dress. The media's expectations are impossible to meet—God's are not. God doesn't expect you to be perfect . . . and neither should you.

If you find yourself bound up by the chains of perfectionism, it's time to ask yourself who you're trying to impress, and why. If you're trying to impress other people, it's time to reconsider your priorities.

Remember this: the expectations that really matter are not society's expectations or your friends' expectations. The expectations that matter are God's expectations, pure and simple. And everything else should take a back seat.

So do your best to please God, and don't worry too much about what other people think. And, when it comes to meeting the unrealistic expectations of our crazy world, forget about trying to meet those unrealistic expectations and concentrate, instead, on living a life that's pleasing to God.

Accept your own imperfections! If you're caught up in the modern-day push toward perfection, grow up . . . and then lighten up on yourself.

I want you to remember what a difference there is between perfection and perfectionism. The former is a Bible truth; the latter may or may not be a human perversion of the truth. I fear that many, in their horror of perfectionism, reject perfection too.

Andrew Murray

God is so inconceivably good. He's not looking for perfection. He already saw it in Christ. He's looking for affection.

Beth Moore

What makes a Christian a Christian is not perfection but forgiveness.

Max Lucado

Bear with the faults of others as you would have them bear with yours.

Phillips Brooks

Better to do something imperfectly than to do nothing perfectly.

Robert Schuller

More from God's Word about Perfectionism

The fear of human opinion disables; trusting in God protects you from that.

Proverbs 29:25 MSG

In thee, O Lord, do I put my trust; let me never be put into confusion.

Psalm 71:1 KJV

Everything God made is good, and nothing should be refused if it is accepted with thanks.

1 Timothy 4:4 NCV

Notes to Yourself about the Problems of Perfectionism

_____

_____

_____

_____

_____

CHAPTER 35

MATERIALISM 101: THE VALUE OF STUFF

Do not love the world or the things in the world. If anyone loves the world, the love of the Father is not in him.

1 John 2:15 NKJV

Is "shop till you drop" your motto? Hopefully not. On the grand stage of a well-lived life, material possessions should play a rather small role. Of course, we all need the basic necessities of life, but once we meet those needs, the piling up of stuff creates more problems than it solves.

Our society is in love with money and the things that money can buy. God is not. God cares about people, not possessions, and so must we. We must, to the best of our abilities, love our neighbors as ourselves, and we must, to the best of our abilities, resist the mighty temptation to place possessions ahead of people.

How much stuff is too much stuff? Well, if your desire for stuff is getting in the way of your desire to know God, then you've got too much stuff—it's as simple as that.

If you find yourself wrapped up in the concerns of the material world, it's time to reorder your priorities by turning your thoughts to more important matters. And, it's time to begin storing up riches that will endure throughout eternity: the spiritual kind. Money, in and of itself, is not evil; worshipping money is. So today, as you prioritize matters of importance in your life, remember that God is almighty, but the dollar is not.

The world wants you to believe that "money and stuff" can buy happiness. Don't believe it! Genuine happiness comes not from money, but from the things that money can't buy—starting, of course, with your relationship to God and His only begotten Son.

The more we stuff ourselves with material pleasures, the less we seem to appreciate life.

Barbara Johnson

A society that pursues pleasure runs the risk of raising expectations ever higher, so that true contentment always lies tantalizingly out of reach.

Philip Yancey and Paul Brand

Outside appearances, things like the clothes you wear or the car you drive, are important to other people but totally unimportant to God. Trust God.

Marie T. Freeman

The Scriptures also reveal warning that if we are consumed with greed, not only do we disobey God, but we will miss the opportunity to allow Him to use us as instruments for others.

Charles Stanley

Why is love of gold more potent than love of souls?

Lottie Moon

More from God's Word about Materialism

And He told them, "Watch out and be on guard against all greed, because one's life is not in the abundance of his possessions."

Luke 12:15 HCSB

For what does it benefit a man to gain the whole world yet lose his life? What can a man give in exchange for his life?

Mark 8:36-37 HCSB

He who trusts in his riches will fall, but the righteous will flourish . . . .

Proverbs 11:28 NKJV

Notes to Yourself about the Need to Avoid the Trap of Materialism

_____

_____

_____

_____

_____

_____

CHAPTER 36

TRUSTING
HIS TIMETABLE

To everything there is a season, a time for every purpose under heaven.

Ecclesiastes 3:1 NKJV

Are you a person in a hurry? If so, you're probably not the only one in your neighborhood. We human beings are, by our very nature, impatient. We are impatient with others, impatient with ourselves, and impatient with our Creator. We want things to happen according to our own timetables, but our Heavenly Father may have other plans. That's why we must learn the art of patience.

All too often, we are unwilling to trust God's perfect timing. We allow ourselves to become apprehensive and anxious as we wait nervously for God to act. Usually, we know what we want, and we know precisely when we want it: right now, if not sooner. But, when God's plans differ from our own, we must train ourselves to trust in His infinite wisdom and in His infinite love.

As people living in a fast-paced world, many of us find that waiting quietly for God is quite troubling. But in our better moments, we realize that patience is not only a virtue, it is also a commandment from the Creator.

Psalm 37:7 makes it clear that we should "Be still before the Lord and wait patiently for Him" (NIV). But ours is a generation that usually places little value on stillness and patience. No matter. God instructs us to be patient in all things, and we must obey Him or suffer the consequences of His displeasure.

We must be patient with our families, with our friends, and with ourselves. We must also be patient with our Heavenly Father as He shapes our world (and our lives) in accordance with His timetable, not our own. And that's as it should be. After all, think how patient God has been with us.

Trust God's timing. God has very big plans in store for you, so trust Him and wait patiently for those plans to unfold. And remember: God's timing is best, so don't allow yourself to become discouraged if things don't work out exactly as you wish. Instead of worrying about your future, entrust it to God. He knows exactly what you need and exactly when you need it.

God never hurries. There are no deadlines against which He must work. To know this is to quiet our spirits and relax our nerves.

A. W. Tozer

God is in no hurry. Compared to the works of mankind, Hi is extremely deliberate. God is not a slave to the human clock.

Charles Swindoll

Waiting on God brings us to the journey's end quicker than our feet.

Mrs. Charles E. Cowman

When we read of the great Biblical leaders, we see that it was not uncommon for God to ask them to wait, not just a day or two, but for years, until God was ready for them to act.

Gloria Gaither

God has a designated time when his promise will be fulfilled and the prayer will be answered.

Jim Cymbala

More from God's Word about God's Timing

I waited patiently for the LORD; and He inclined to me, and heard my cry.

Psalm 40:1 NKJV

Wait on the LORD; be of good courage, and He shall strengthen your heart; wait, I say, on the LORD!

Psalm 27:14 NKJV

He said to them, "It is not for you to know times or periods that the Father has set by His own authority."

Acts 1:7 HCSB

Notes to Yourself about the Importance of Trusting God's Timing

_____

_____

_____

_____

_____

_____

CHAPTER 37

HAVE A HUMBLE HEART

Clothe yourselves with humility toward one another, because God resists the proud, but gives grace to the humble.

1 Peter 5:5 HCSB

We have heard the phrases on countless occasions: "He's a self-made man," or "she's a self-made woman." In truth, none of us are self-made. We all owe countless debts that we can never repay.

Our first debt, of course, is to our Father in heaven—who has given us everything—and to His Son who sacrificed His own life so that we might live eternally. We are also indebted to ancestors, parents, teachers, friends, spouses, family members, coworkers, fellow believers . . . and the list, of course, goes on.

As Christians, we have a profound reason to be humble: We have been refashioned and saved by Jesus Christ, and that salvation came not because of our own good works but because of God's grace. Thus, we are not "self-made"; we are "God-made" and "Christ-saved." How, then, can we be boastful? The answer, of course, is that, if we are honest with ourselves and with our God, we simply can't be boastful . . . we must, instead, be eternally grateful and exceedingly humble.

Humility is not, in most cases, a naturally-occurring human trait. Most of us, it seems, are more than willing to stick out our chests and say, "Look at me; I did that!" But in our better moments, in the quiet moments when we search the depths of our own hearts, we know better. Whatever "it" is, God did that, not us. And He deserves the credit.

Do you value humility above status? If so, God will smile upon your endeavors. But if you value status above humility, you're inviting God's displeasure. In short, humility pleases God; pride does not.

If you know who you are in Christ, your personal ego is not an issue.

Beth Moore

Jesus had a humble heart. If He abides in us, pride will never dominate our lives.

Billy Graham

The humble person will not be thinking humility: He will not be thinking about himself at all.

C. S. Lewis

That some of my hymns have been dictated by the blessed Holy Spirit I have no doubt; and that others have been the result of deep meditation I know to be true; but that the poet has any right to claim special merit for himself is certainly presumptuous.

Fanny Crosby

Humility is an attitude. The Lord is high and lifted up, and we are supposed to take a position of lowliness.

Franklin Graham

More from God's Word about Humility

Humble yourselves therefore under the mighty hand of God, so that He may exalt you in due time, casting all your care upon Him, because He cares about you.

1 Peter 5:6-7 HCSB

You will save the humble people; but Your eyes are on the haughty, that You may bring them down.

2 Samuel 22:28 NKJV

Do nothing out of rivalry or conceit, but in humility consider others as more important than yourselves.

Philippians 2:3 HCSB

 ## Notes to Yourself about the Rewards of Humility

_____

_____

_____

_____

_____

_____

CHAPTER 38

AIM HIGH

Live full lives, full in the fullness of God. God can do anything, you know—far more than you could ever imagine or guess or request in your wildest dreams! He does it not by pushing us around but by working within us, his Spirit deeply and gently within us.

Ephesians 3:19-20 MSG

How big are you willing to dream? Are you willing to entertain the possibility that God has big plans in store for you? Or are you convinced that your future is so dim that you'd better wear night goggles? Well, if you're a believer in the One from Galilee, you have an incredibly bright future ahead of you . . . here on earth and in heaven. That's why you have every right to dream big.

Concentration camp survivor Corrie ten Boom observed, "Every experience God gives us, every person he brings into our lives, is the perfect preparation for the future that only he can see." These words apply to you.

Are you excited about the opportunities of today and thrilled by the possibilities of tomorrow? Do you confidently expect God to lead you to a place of abundance, peace, and joy? And, when your days on earth are over, do you expect to receive the priceless gift of eternal life? If you trust God's promises, and if you have welcomed God's Son into your heart, then you believe that your future is intensely and eternally bright.

It takes courage to dream big dreams. You will discover that courage when you do three things: accept the past, trust God to handle the future, and make the most of the time He has given you today.

Nothing is too difficult for God, and no dreams are too big for Him—not even yours. So start living—and dreaming—accordingly.

Making your dreams come true requires work. John Maxwell writes "The gap between your vision and your present reality can only be filled through a commitment to maximize your potential." Enough said.

The future lies all before us. Shall it only be a slight advance upon what we usually do? Ought it not to be a bound, a leap forward to altitudes of endeavor and success undreamed of before?

Annie Armstrong

Sometimes our dreams were so big that it took two people to dream them.

Marie T. Freeman

You cannot out-dream God.

John Eldredge

May your day be fashioned with joy, sprinkled with dreams, and touched by the miracle of love.

Barbara Johnson

What you get by reaching your goals is not nearly as important as what you become by reaching them.

Zig Ziglar

More from God's Word about Dreams

Now may the God of hope fill you with all joy and peace in believing, so that you may overflow with hope by the power of the Holy Spirit.

Romans 15:13 HCSB

Where there is no vision, the people perish . . . .

Proverbs 29:18 KJV

As we have therefore opportunity, let us do good unto all men, especially unto them who are of the household of faith.

Galatians 6:10 KJV

Notes to Yourself about Your Dreams

_____

_____

_____

_____

_____

_____

CHAPTER 39

GOD'S SURPRISING PLANS

Who is the person who fears the Lord? He will show him the way he should choose. He will live a good life, and his descendants will inherit the land.

The Bible makes it clear: God's got a plan—a whopper of a plan—and you play a vitally important role in it. But here's the catch: God won't force His plans upon you; you've got to figure things out for yourself . . . or not.

As a Christian, you should ask yourself this question: "How closely can I make my plans match God's plans?" The more closely you manage to follow the path that God intends for your life, the better.

Do you have questions or concerns about the future? Take them to God in prayer. Do you have hopes and expectations? Talk to God about your dreams. Are you carefully planning for the days and weeks ahead? Consult God as you establish your priorities. Turn every concern over to your Heavenly Father, and sincerely seek His guidance—

prayerfully, earnestly, and often. Then, listen for His answers . . . and trust the answers that He gives.

Sometimes, God's plans are crystal clear, but other times, He may lead you through the wilderness before He delivers you to the Promised Land. So be patient, keep praying, and keep seeking His will for your life. When you do, you'll be amazed at the marvelous things that an all-powerful, all-knowing God can do.

Waiting faithfully for God's plan to unfold is more important than understanding God's plan. Ruth Bell Graham once said, " When I am dealing with an all-powerful, all-knowing God, I, as a mere mortal, must offer my petitions not only with persistence, but also with patience. Someday I'll know why." Even when you can't understand God's plans, you must trust Him and never lose faith!

When the dream of our heart is one that God has planted there, a strange happiness flows into us. At that moment, all of the spiritual resources of the universe are released to help us. Our praying is then at one with the will of God and becomes a channel for the Creator's purposes for us and our world.

Catherine Marshall

God will not permit any troubles to come upon us unless He has a specific plan by which great blessing can come out of the difficulty.

Peter Marshall

In God's plan, God is the standard for perfection. We don't compare ourselves to others; they are just as fouled up as we are. The goal is to be like him; anything less is inadequate.

Max Lucado

God is preparing you as his chosen arrow. As yet your shaft is hidden in his quiver, in the shadows, but, at the precise moment, he will reach for you and launch you to that place of his appointment.

Charles Swindoll

169

More from God's Word about God's Plans

"I say this because I know what I am planning for you," says the Lord. "I have good plans for you, not plans to hurt you. I will give you hope and a good future."

Jeremiah 29:11 NCV

A man's heart plans his way, but the Lord directs his steps.

Proverbs 16:9 NKJV

We know that all things work together for the good of those who love God: those who are called according to His purpose.

Romans 8:28 HCSB

 ## Notes to Yourself about God's Plans for You

_____

_____

_____

_____

_____

_____

CHAPTER 40

THIS IS THE DAY . . .

This is the day which the Lord hath made; we will rejoice and be glad in it.

Psalm 118:24 KJV

The familiar words of Psalm 118 remind us that today, like every day, is a priceless gift from God. What do you expect from the day ahead? Are you expecting God to do wonderful things, or are you living beneath a cloud of apprehension and doubt? Do you expect God to use you in unexpected ways, or do you expect another uneventful day to pass with little fanfare? As a thoughtful believer, the answer to these questions should be obvious.

C. H. Spurgeon, the renowned 19th-century English clergyman, advised, "Rejoicing is clearly a spiritual command. To ignore it, I need to remind you, is disobedience." As Christians, we are called by our Creator to live abundantly, prayerfully, and joyfully. To do otherwise is to squander His spiritual gifts.

If you're a thoughtful Christian, then you're a thankful Christian. And because of your faith, you can face the

171

inevitable challenges and disappointments of each day armed with the joy of Christ and the promise of salvation.

So whatever this day holds for you, begin it and end it with God as your partner and Christ as your Savior. And throughout the day, give thanks to the One who created you and saved you. God's love for you is infinite—accept it joyfully and be thankful.

Today, like every other day, provides countless opportunities to serve God and to worship Him. But, if we turn our backs on our Creator, or if we simply become too busy to acknowledge His greatness, we do a profound disservice to ourselves, to our families, and to our world.

When we truly walk with God throughout our day, life slowly starts to fall into place.

Bill Hybels

Every day of our lives we make choices about how we're going to live that day.

Luci Swindoll

Wherever you are, be all there. Live to the hilt every situation you believe to be the will of God.

Jim Elliot

Today is mine. Tomorrow is none of my business. If I peer anxiously into the fog of the future, I will strain my spiritual eyes so that I will not see clearly what is required of me now.

Elisabeth Elliot

All our life is like a day of celebration for us; we are convinced, in fact, that God is always everywhere. We work while singing; we sail while reciting hymns; we accomplish all other occupations of life while praying.

St. Clement of Alexandria

More from God's Word about Today

I must work the works of Him who sent Me while it is day; the night is coming when no one can work.

John 9:4 NKJV

So think clearly and exercise self-control. Look forward to the special blessings that will come to you at the return of Jesus Christ.

1 Peter 1:13 NLT

So teach us to number our days, that we may gain a heart of wisdom.

Psalm 90:12 NKJV

Notes to Yourself about the Need to Celebrate Today

_____

_____

_____

_____

_____

_____